North Cascades National Park Complex Glacier Mass Balance Monitoring Annual Report, Water Year 2009

North Coast and Cascades Network

Natural Resource Technical Report NPS/NCCN/NRTR—2011/483

Jon Riedel, Ph.D

North Coast and Cascades Network
National Park Service
North Cascades National Park Service Complex
810 State Route 20
Sedro-Woolley, WA 98284

Michael Larrabee

North Coast and Cascades Network
National Park Service
North Cascades National Park Service Complex
810 State Route 20
Sedro-Woolley, WA 98284

August 2011

U.S. Department of the Interior
National Park Service
Natural Resource Stewardship and Science
Fort Collins, Colorado

The National Park Service, Natural Resource Stewardship and Science office in Fort Collins, Colorado publishes a range of reports that address natural resource topics of interest and applicability to a broad audience in the National Park Service and others in natural resource management, including scientists, conservation and environmental constituencies, and the public.

The Natural Resource Technical Report Series is used to disseminate results of scientific studies in the physical, biological, and social sciences for both the advancement of science and the achievement of the National Park Service mission. The series provides contributors with a forum for displaying comprehensive data that are often deleted from journals because of page limitations.

All manuscripts in the series receive the appropriate level of peer review to ensure that the information is scientifically credible, technically accurate, appropriately written for the intended audience, and designed and published in a professional manner.

This report received informal peer review by subject-matter experts who were not directly involved in the collection, analysis, or reporting of the data. Data in this report were collected and analyzed using methods based on established, peer-reviewed protocols and were analyzed and interpreted within the guidelines of the protocols.

This report is available from The North Coast and Cascades Network (http://science.nature.nps.gov/im/units/nccn/reportpubs.cfm) and the Natural Resource Publications Management website (http://www.nature.nps.gov/publications/nrpm/).

Please cite this publication as:

Riedel, J., and M. A. Larrabee. 2011. North Cascades National Park Complex glacier mass balance monitoring annual report, Water year 2009: North Coast and Cascades Network. Natural Resource Technical Report NPS/NCCN/NRTR—2011/483. National Park Service, Fort Collins, Colorado.

NPS 168/109433, August 2011

Contents

Contents (continued)

Figures

Tables

Abstract

Glaciers cover approximately 109 km^2 in North Cascades National Park Service Complex (NOCA), and are a high-priority Vital Sign in the North Coast and Cascades Network monitoring plan because they are sensitive, dramatic indicators of climate change and drivers of aquatic and terrestrial ecosystems. Since 1993, seasonal volume changes at four NOCA glaciers have been monitored by tracking seasonal surface mass balance at four-to-five sites/glacier.

Water year 2009 had a slightly below average winter accumulation, and Noisy and Sandalee glaciers had a winter mass balance of about 3 ±0.2 m water equivalent (w.e.). Higher elevation Silver and North Klawatti glaciers had lower winter balances of 2.5 ±0.2 m w.e. and 2 ±0.26 m w.e., respectively. Summer melting on all four glaciers ranked among the top three melt seasons since 1993, with North Klawatti Glacier's summer mass balance exceeding -4 ±0.47 m w.e. The combination of an average winter mass balance and a very negative summer mass balances drove net mass balance negative for the seventh consecutive year on all four glaciers. North Klawatti Glacier had the lowest net mass balance at -2.2 ±0.36 m w.e, while east-side Sandalee Glacier had the least negative net mass balance at -1.3 ±0.44 m w.e.

Negative mass balances for all four glaciers in water year 2009 strengthened the negative cumulative balance trend since 1993 for all four glaciers. Noisy, North Klawatti, and Sandalee glaciers have cumulative net mass balances of about -15 m w.e., whereas higher-elevation Silver Glacier had a cumulative balance of -9 m w.e. Since 1993 the average annual melt rate for all four glaciers has increased by about 10% (1 m w.e.).

High rates of summer melt and average snowpack led to significant glacial contribution to streamflow at NOCA. In four major watersheds glaciers contributed 472 M m^3 (120 B gallons) of water to park lakes and streams. In Thunder Creek, glaciers provided about 44% of total summer runoff, whereas in the more arid, less glaciated Ross Lake basin glaciers contributed about 10%.

Ten-year remapping of Sandalee and Silver glaciers was completed in 2009 and led to significant adjustment to the base maps used for integration of point (stake) measurement to the entire glacier. Both glaciers had net vertical surface decline exceeding 15 m. Back-adjustment of data from 2000 - 2009 with the new hypsometry data led to a significant decreases in cumulative balance of -3.30 m on Silver Glacier and -5.83 m on Sandalee Glacier.

Acknowledgments

Measurement of mass balance on four glaciers, adjustment of base maps, and administration of this project were only possible through the concerted effort of a large group of individuals. Field measurements were supported by Stephen Dorsch, Rob Burrows, Sharon Brady, Jeff Weyand, Hugh Anthony, and Benjamin Wright. Rob Burrows and Erin Pettit contributed valuable time, equipment, and expertise to the remapping of Silver and Sandalee glaciers. We also want to thank Sarah Welch, Ron Holmes, Viki Gonzales, Mark Huff, and Jack Oelfke for their administrative support. We would also like to recognize the peer-reviewers who substantially improved this report, including Mark Huff, Rebecca Lofgren, Ashley Rawhouser, Regina Rochefort and Barbara Samora.

Introduction

The National Park Service began long-term monitoring of mass balance of glaciers within North Cascades National Park Complex (NOCA) in 1993. Monitoring includes direct field measurements of accumulation and melt to estimate volume gained and lost on a seasonal and water-year basis. Noisy Creek, Silver Creek, and North Klawatti Glaciers have been monitored at NOCA since 1993 and a fourth glacier, Sandalee, since 1995 (Figure 1). The purpose of this report is to describe field work and summarize data collected for water year 2009.

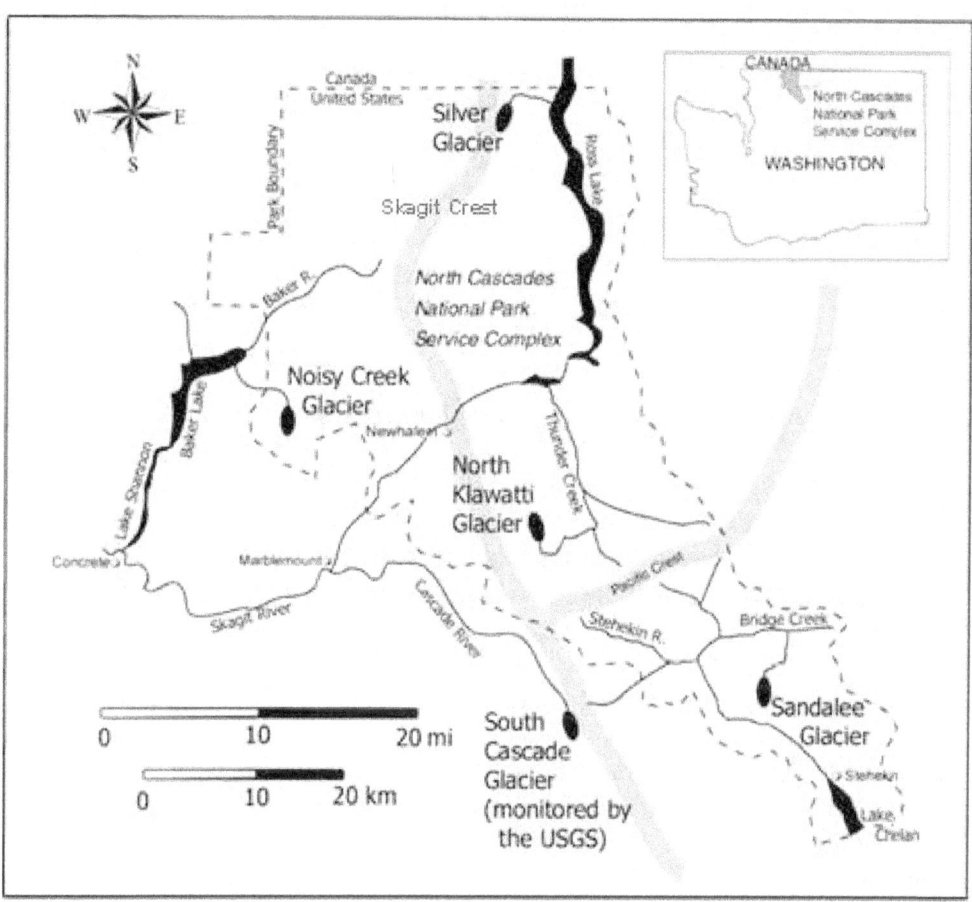

Figure 1. Locations of monitored glaciers and major hydrologic divides in the North Cascades (Riedel et al., 2008).

Glaciers are a significant resource of the Cascade Range in Washington State. North Cascades National Park contained 316 glaciers that covered 109 km^2 in a 1998 inventory (Granshaw 2002). They are integral components of the region's hydrologic, ecologic, and geologic systems. Glacial melt water delivery peaks during the hot, dry summers in the Pacific Northwest, buffering the region's aquatic ecosystems from seasonal and interannual droughts. Aquatic ecosystems, endangered species such as salmon, bull trout and western cutthroat trout, and the hydroelectric and agricultural industries benefit from the seasonal and interannual stability glaciers impart to the region's hydrologic systems.

Glaciers significantly change the distribution of aquatic and terrestrial habitat through their advance and retreat. They directly influence aquatic habitat by the amount of cold, turbid melt water and fine-grained sediment they release. Glaciers also indirectly influence habitat through their effect on nutrient cycling and microclimate. Many of the subalpine and alpine plant communities in the park flourish on landforms and soils created by glaciers within the last century. Further, glaciers are habitat to a number of species, and are the sole habitat for ice worms (*Mesenchytraeus solifugus*) and certain species of springtails (Collembola) (Hartzell, 2003).

Glaciers are also important indicators of regional and global climate change. At North Cascades National Park, geologic mapping data, unpublished maps made by from Austin Post, and a 1998 inventory (Granshaw and Fountain 2006) indicate that glacier area has declined ~50% in the last 100 years.

The four index glaciers monitored represent varying characteristics of glaciers found in the North Cascades, including altitude, aspect, and geographic location in relation to the main hydrologic crests (Figure 1). The glaciers selected drain into four major watersheds from NOCA and represent a 1000 meter range in altitude from the terminus of Noisy Glacier to the top of Silver Glacier.

Four broad goals are identified to monitor glaciers as important Vital Signs of the ecological health of NOCA:

1) Monitor range of variation and trends in volume of NOCA glaciers;
2) Relate glacier changes to status of aquatic and terrestrial ecosystems;
3) Link glacier observations to research on climate and ecosystem change; and
4) Share information on glaciers with the public and professionals.

Objectives identified to reach the program goals include:

> Collect a network of point surface mass balance measurements sufficient to define elevation versus balance relationships to estimate glacier averaged winter, summer and net balance for all index glaciers.
> Map and quantify surface elevation changes of all index glaciers every 10 years.
> Identify trends in glacier mass balance.
> Inventory margin position, area, condition, and equilibrium line altitudes of all park glaciers every 20 years.
> Monitor glacier melt, water discharge, and glacier area/volume change.
> Share data and information gathered in this program with a variety of audiences from school children to colleagues and the professional community.

Methods

Mass balance measurement methods used in this project generally follow procedures established during 45 years of research on the South Cascade Glacier (SCG) by the USGS-Water Resources Division (Meier 1961, Meier and Tangborn 1965, Meier et al. 1971, Tangborn et al. 1971, Krimmel 1994, 1995, 1996, 1996a). They are very similar to those used around the world, as described by Ostrem and Stanley (1969), Paterson (1981), and Ostrem and Brugman (1991). Detailed procedures are outlined in Riedel et al. (2008), *Long Term Monitoring of Small Glaciers at North Cascades National Park* (NPS/NCCN/NRR-2008/000).

Measurement System

We use a two-season stratigraphic approach to calculate mass gained (winter balance) and mass lost (summer balance) on a seasonal basis. Summation of these measurements allows for calculation of the net mass balance of a given glacier during the course of one water year (October 1-September 30). Measurements of accumulation and melt are made at around the same time every year in early spring and fall at approximately the same locations. Due to weather and logistical limitations, the actual maximum and minimum mass balance may not be recorded. Differences between actual events and the times of measurement are assumed to be negligible.

Winter balance is calculated from snow depth and bulk density measurements. Snow depth is measured at five to 10 points near four to 10 locations along the centerline of the glacier (ablation stakes) and other selected locations, resulting in 20-50 measurements per glacier. Snow density on each glacier is measured at the ablation stake location which is closest to the mid-point altitude of the glacier. When not directly measured, the average measured density of the spring snowpack since 1993 (0.5 +/- 0.05) is used. This value is also compared to values measured independently at SNOTEL[1] sites by the Natural Resource Conservation Service and at South Cascade Glacier by the U.S. Geological Survey.

Ablation stakes are used to measure summer balance. Stakes are placed in late April/early May when snow depth is probed for winter balance. Measurements of surface level change against the stakes are made in early to mid-summer and in late September to early October on each glacier. The change in ice, snow and firn elevation against the stake, while accounting for changes in the densities of firn and glacier ice, indicates the mass lost at the surface during the summer season (summer balance).

Oblique aerial photographs are taken of each index glacier as a record of change in area, surface elevation, equilibrium line altitude, and snow, firn and ice coverage. These color photographs are taken in early spring and late summer.

---

[1] SNOTEL stations provide real-time snow and climate data in the mountainous regions of the Western United States using automated remote sensing. The Natural Resource Conservation Service operates and maintains SNOTEL stations located within North Cascade National Park (http://www.wcc.nrcs.usda.gov/snotel/Washington/washington.html).

Glacial Meltwater Discharge

Glacier contribution to summer streamflow is calculated annually in four park watersheds: Baker River, Thunder Creek, Ross Lake, and Stehekin River (Figure 1). The summer melt season is defined as the period between May 1 and September 30. These dates approximately coincide with winter and summer balance field measurements and the beginning and end of ablation season. Selection of these dates means that runoff estimates from glaciers include snow as well as firn and ice.

A simple model is used to estimate glacier contributions to summer stream flow, and is based on the strong relationship between summer melt and altitude. This relationship is constrained by data from 18 melt stakes on four glaciers that spans 1000 m. Vertical melt at a given elevation from this curve is then multiplied by glacier area in 50m bands derived by GIS, then summed for each watershed. The fraction of glacial meltwater to total summer runoff is determined at USGS gage sites on each river.

Glacier Mapping and Balance Adjustments

Accurate glacier maps are an important component of this monitoring program. Maps are used to assess area changes, advance/ retreat of termini, surface elevation/ volume changes, and to provide accurate base maps for mass balance calculations.

The area-altitude distribution of the four index glaciers are remapped every 10 years using vertical aerial photographs and high precision GPS point data. The original maps for Silver and Sandalee glaciers were made in 1994 and 1996 based on photogrammetry from stereo air photos. The contractor used few control points and relied on USGS Quad coordinates and elevations. To improve the maps, benchmarks were installed and surveyed using a survey grade GPS in summer of 2005 and 2006.

In addition to remapping of index glacier hypsometry every 10 years, the surface area of all park glaciers are remapped every 20 years. The park-wide inventory is based on vertical aerial photographs and was last completed in 1998 (Granshaw and Fountain 2006).

1993 to 2009 Record

In this report, we present data measured in 2009 and compare it to data collected from 1993-2008, using the methods described in Riedel et al. (2008). We present 17-year comparisons of winter, summer, net, and cumulative glacial balance, and summer glacial meltwater contributions to the Thunder Creek, Ross Lake and Baker and Stehekin River watersheds. A summary of the first decade of mass balance results was published in 2001 (Pelto and Riedel 2001).

Results

Measurement Error

Sources of error in mass balance estimates are calculated on an annual, stake-by-stake, and glacier-by-glacier basis. Errors associated with winter, summer, and net balance estimates in water year 2009 were within the range of values reported since 1993 (Table 1). Net balance error on Silver Glacier remained the highest of all four glaciers at ±0.56 m w.e.

Table 1. Calculated error for Water Year 2009 mass balance calculations for NOCA index glaciers, with period of record averages in parenthesis.

Glacier	Average Stake Error (m w.e.)		
	Winter Balance	Summer Balance	Net Balance
Noisy	±0.22 (0.20)	±0.25 (0.26)	±0.33 (0.31)
North Klawatti	±0.20 (0.21)	±0.47 (0.31)	±0.36 (0.32)
Sandalee	±0.20 (0.19)	±0.39 (0.26)	±0.44 (0.33)
Silver	±0.26 (0.26)	±0.49 (0.33)	±0.56 (0.42)

Winter and Summer Balance

Winter accumulation from October 2008 to April 2009 was average at Noisy (+3.14 m w.e.) and Sandalee (+3 m w.e.) glaciers, and about 15% below average at Silver (+2 m w.e.) and North Klawatti (+2.5 m w.e.) glaciers (Figure 2).

Summer melt in 2009 for the four index glaciers was 120% of average determined during the past 17 years. At North Klawatti and Noisy Glaciers the average melt exceeded 4 m, with melting at low elevation stakes of 7.5 m w.e. and 4.8 m w.e., respectively.

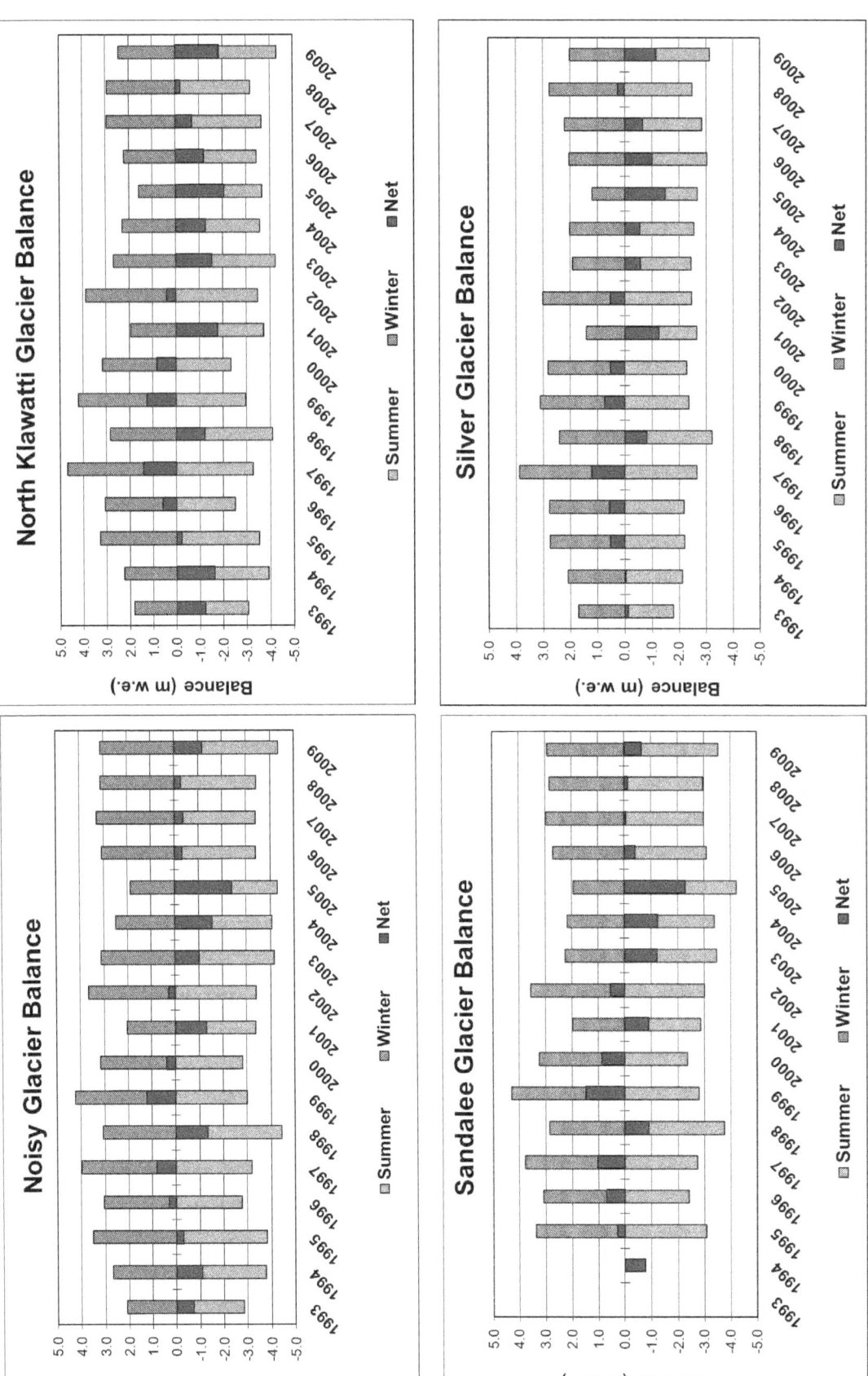

Figure 2. Winter, summer and net mass balances for each glacier by water year.

Net Balance

Annual net mass balances for four NOCA index glaciers were negative in water year 2009 (Figures 2 and 3). This year was the seventh consecutive year where all four glaciers lost more mass to summer melting than they gained in the previous winter. North Klawatti Glacier had the most negative mass balance (-2.20 ±0.36 m w.e.), while Sandalee Glacier had the least negative balance (-1.3 ±0.44 m w.e.).

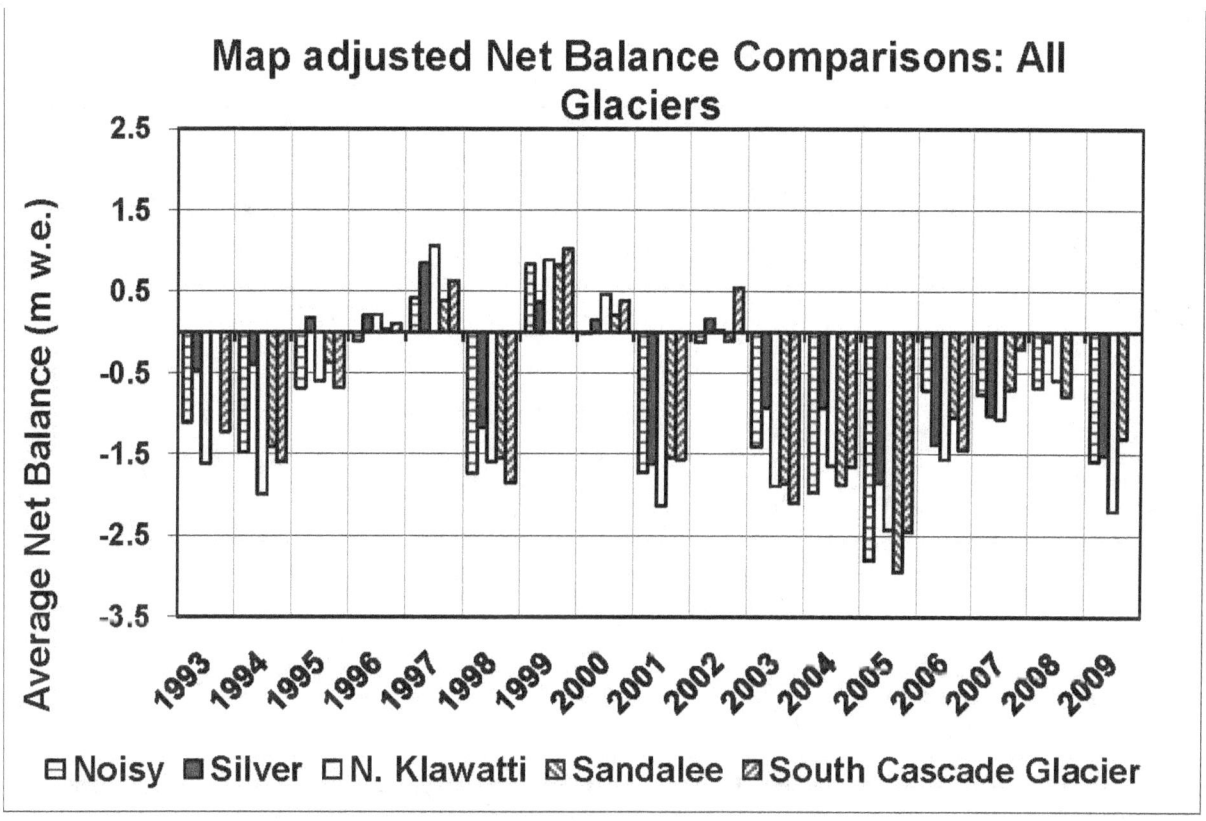

Figure 3. Net mass balance comparisons for each glacier by water year.

Cumulative Balance

Seven consecutive years of negative net mass balance for all four glaciers has driven cumulative balances deeply into negative territory (Figure 4). Since 1993, the cumulative balance for all glaciers ranges from -16.67 m w.e. (North Klawatti) to -9.49 m w.e. (Silver). After a short period of modest volume increase between 1996 and 2003, NOCA glaciers have resumed a negative long-term trend. Water years 2000-2009 showed substantial mass loss for all glaciers, with average net vertical change of 11.67 m w.e. and total volume loss of 32 M m^3 w.e.

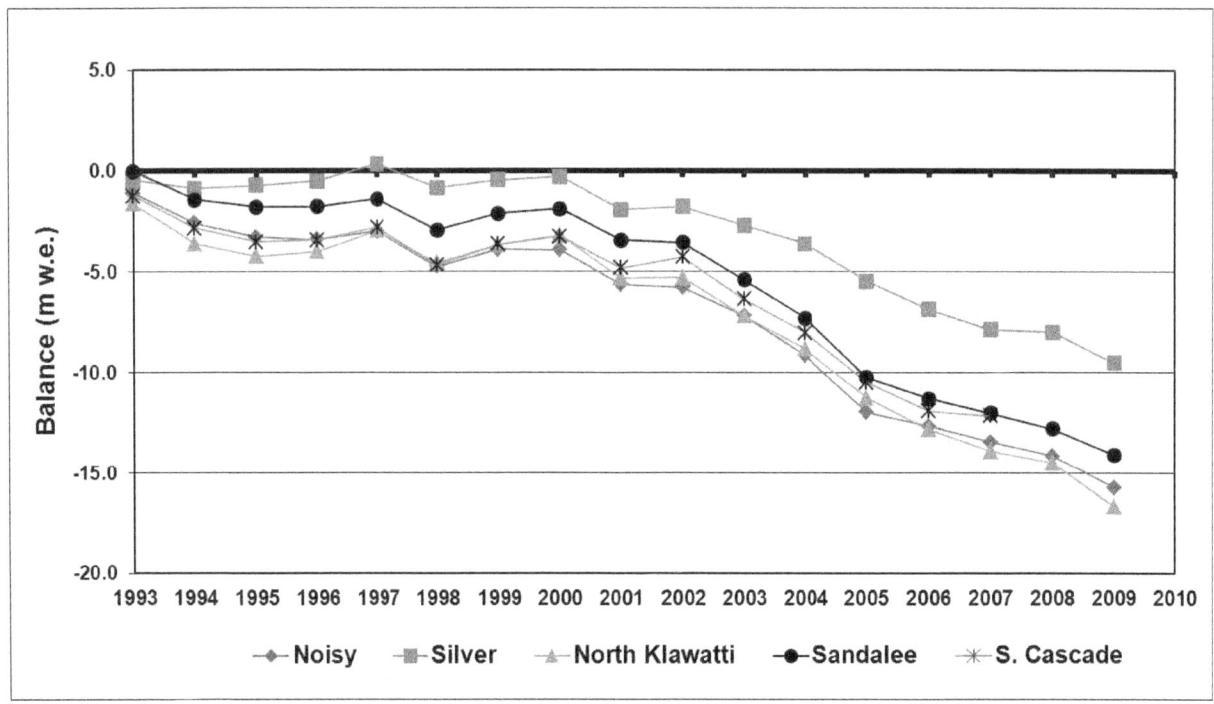

Figure 4. Cumulative balance for each glacier by water year. Sandalee and Silver glacier curves are map-adjusted.

Glacial Contribution to Streamflow

Glacial contribution to runoff was above average in all watersheds due to above average summer melt and below average winter snow accumulation. Both Silver and Sandalee glaciers released more meltwater this water year than in any other year since 1993. Depending on the basin, glacial contribution to summer streamflow was 1-12 percent above normal (Table 2 and Figure 5).

Table 2. Glacial contribution to summer streamflow for four NOCA watersheds. Meltwater contributions are provided for each index glacier and from all glaciers within the watershed. In parenthesis is percent of total watershed area that is glaciated. Average, minimum and maximum values are calculated from 1993-2009 data, with the exception of Stehekin River watershed (1995-2009).

Site (% area glaciated)	May-September Runoff (million cubic meters)				Percent Glacial of Total Summer Runoff			
	2009	average	min	max	2009	average	min	max
Baker River Watershed								
Noisy Creek Glacier	2.3	1.9	1.5	2.4				
All glaciers (6)	103.9	87.1	61.8	107.5	9.2	9.5	5.6	14.6
Thunder Creek Watershed								
North Klawatti Glacier	6.3	5.1	3.4	6.3				
All glaciers (13)	165.7	124.6	88.5	165.7	44.0	32.3	20.7	47.7
Stehekin River Watershed								
Sandalee Glacier	0.7	0.6	0.4	0.8				
All glaciers(3)	105.9	89.2	63.7	108.7	14.0	10.7	5.4	22.9
Ross Lake Watershed								
Silver Glacier	1.4	1.2	0.9	1.6				
All glaciers (1)	96.7	80.1	58.4	99.3	6.9	5.7	2.5	13.5

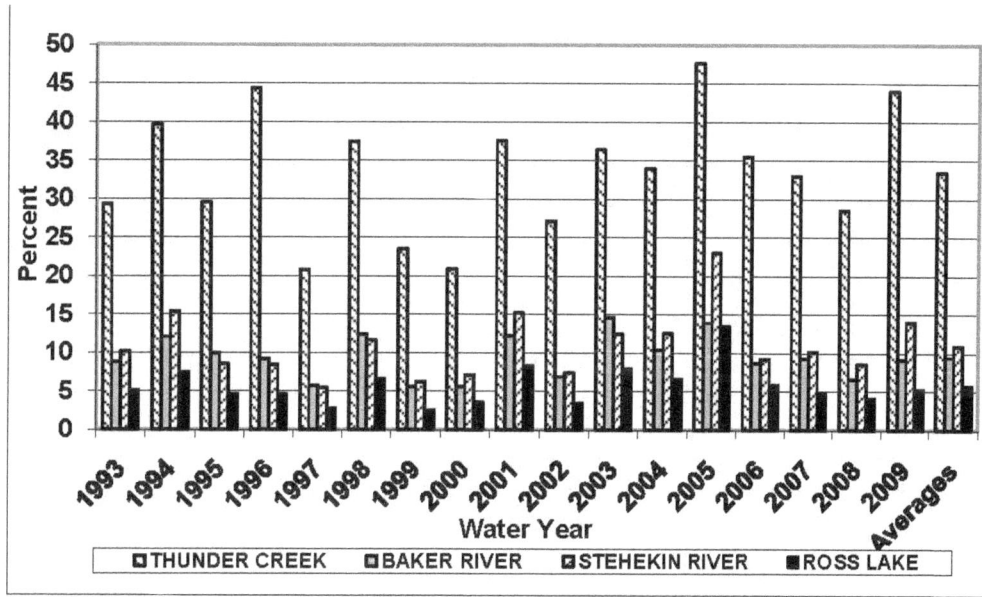

Figure 5. Total summer glacier meltwater contributions for the four watersheds containing a glacier monitored by NOCA.

9

Silver and Sandalee Glacier Balance Adjustments

Tracking glacial movement via contour maps and digital elevation models (DEMs) are important components of this monitoring program. In 2009, corrections were made to the original maps and new maps were created for Silver and Sandalee glaciers (Figures 6 and 7). The original base maps were adjusted using improved spatial data resulting from surveyed benchmarks that were installed 2005 and 2006. Remapping of Silver and Sandalee glaciers hypsometry was based on aerial photographs taken in 2004 and 2006 and high precision GPS point data. Provisional maps for North Klawatti and Noisy glaciers will be finalized in 2011.

For more accurate and consistent mass balance results the balance calculations were redone with this new information from both sets of new maps. From 1993-2000, Silver and Sandalee mass balance calculations were based on the corrected 1993/1996 maps. From 2001-2009, Silver and Sandalee mass balance calculations are based on the updated maps.

Comparison between corrected 1993/1996 maps and the new 2004/2006 maps indicate the area of Silver Glacier decreased 16% in this period, while the area of Sandalee Glacier was reduced by 5.4%. North Klawatti and Noisy glacier areas decreased by 6.6 and 8%, respectively. Both glaciers had net vertical surface changes exceeding 15m.

Back-adjustment of data from 2001 -2009 resulted in significant decreases in cumulative balance and annual net balance. Cumulative balance decreased by -3.30 m w.e. on Silver Glacier and -5.83 m w.e. on Sandalee glacier.

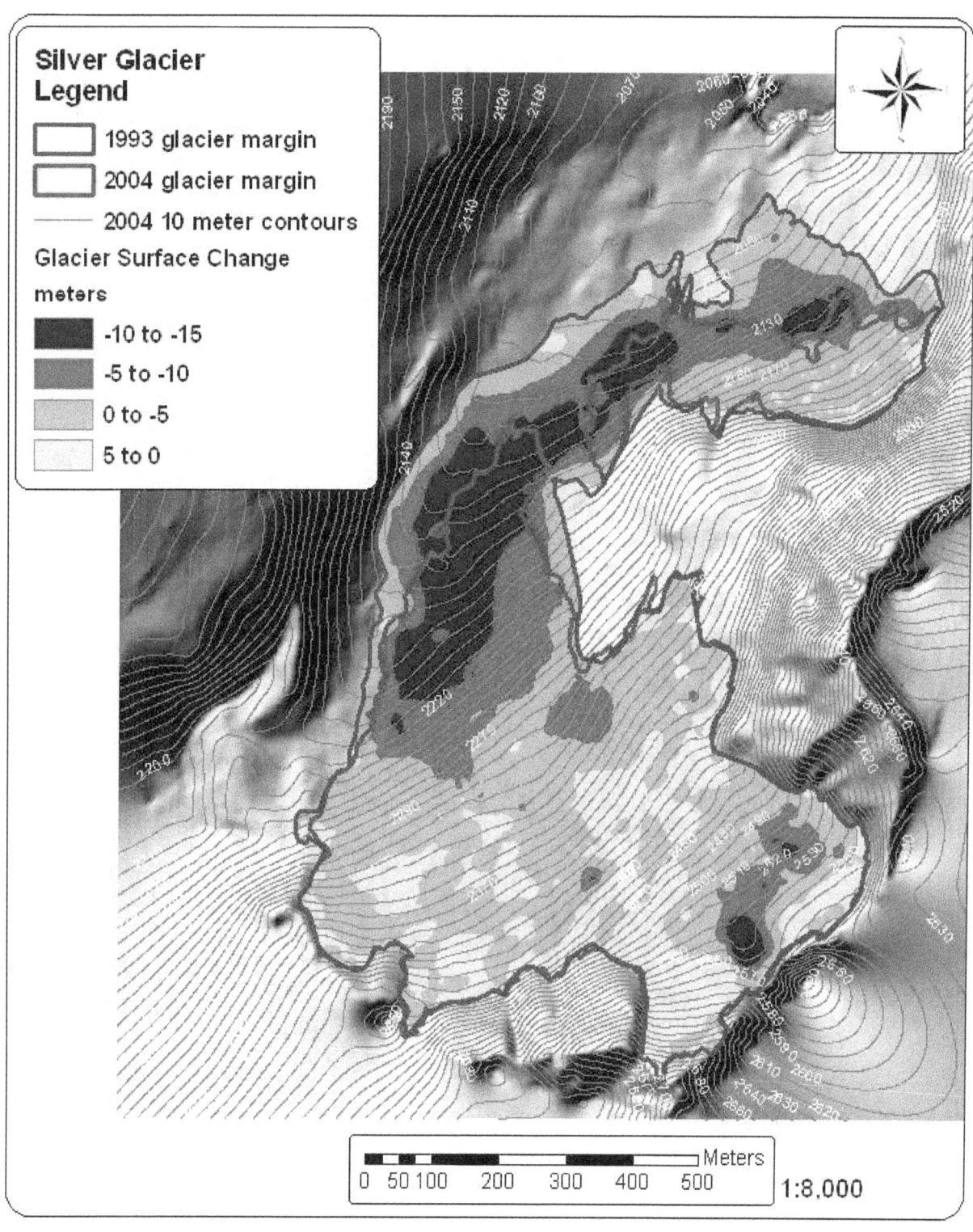

Figure 6. Silver Glacier comparison of 1993 adjusted reference map and 2004/2005 balance map. Glacier surface elevation change is the difference between the 1993 surface (photogrammetry) and 2004/2005 surfaces from photogrammetry and GPS.

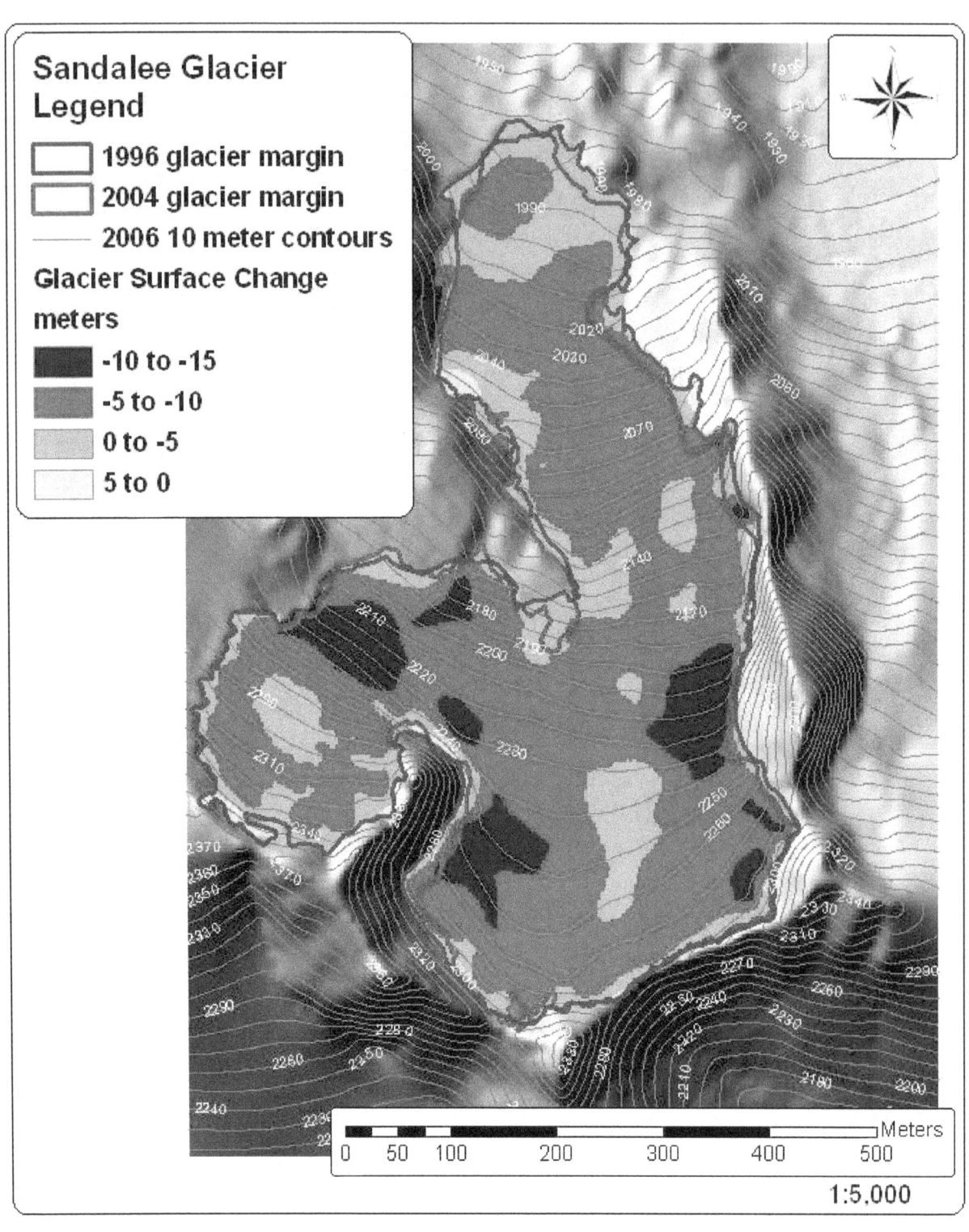

Figure 7. Sandalee Glacier comparison of 1996 adjusted reference map and 2004/2006 balance map. Glacier surface elevation change is the difference between the 1996 surface (photogrammetry) and 2006 July surface from a GPS survey led by Erin Pettit.

Aerial Imagery

The strongly negative mass balances observed in water year 2009 provided a good opportunity to document surface conditions on Silver Glacier (Figure 9). Photographs for Silver Glacier taken during the 2009 spring and fall field visits reveal the dramatic seasonal changes associated with the deposition and melt of 7 m of snowfall in winter 2008-2009. In contrast, the summer image shows the flat, crevasse-free terminus of this glacier, which is indicative of a glacier that is in rapid retreat.

Figure 8. Silver Glacier from the east, April 20, 2009.

Figure 9. Silver Glacier from the north, September 21, 2009.

Discussion

Measurement Error

Silver Glacier had the highest reported net mass balance error at ±0.56 m w.e. in water year 2009. This value was due to highly variable winter accumulation probe measurements on the high elevation upper glacier, caused by wind drifting and a lack of summer surface layer development and low snow temperature. It was also caused by a relatively large summer balance error likely associated with stake sinking and late season ablation.

Sources of error include measurements of snow depth, stake height, snow density, stake/probe position and altitude, and non-synchronous measurements with actual maximum and minimum balances. A thorough discussion of error is provided by Riedel et al. (2008).

Mayo et al. (1972) estimate that surface mass balance measurements account for about 90 percent of actual mass balance because they do not account for subglacial melting and other minor processes of ablation and accumulation. Quantifying these unmeasured variables is accomplished by annual estimates of error and map adjustments to cumulative balance, as discussed below.

Mass Balance

Winter accumulation on the four glaciers in water year 2009 was within the range of those observed at each glacier since 1993, which vary from a gain of 1.5-4.5m w.e. On the relatively small glaciers at NOCA, winter accumulation does not always increase systematically with elevation, although that trend is evident at North Klawatti Glacier, the largest monitored at 1.46 km^2. Strong winds and snow avalanching weaken the relationship between elevation and winter accumulation on smaller Noisy, Silver and Sandalee Glaciers. On Silver Glacier, prevailing westerly winds controlled by local topography consistently deposit a large drift on lower Silver Glacier (Figure 9), which results in a more positive winter balance at 2300 m elevation than higher on the glacier.

Winter balance data reflect the strong climate gradients in the park. A general decrease in accumulation averaged over the area of a given glacier is observed from west (Noisy Glacier) to east, with distance from the Pacific moisture source. Regional spatial mass balance patterns are discussed in detail in a 2001 summary report (Pelto and Riedel 2001).

As with winter balance, summer balance on small glaciers at NOCA is strongly controlled by shadows that slow melting and weaken the relationship between summer balance and elevation. For example, Sandalee Glacier stake 3 at 2100 m elevation typically has more melting than stake 4 at 2000 m elevation because of strong radiation shading of the lower glacier by McGregor Mountain.

Unlike glaciers at MORA and OLYM, those at NOCA are found on crystalline rocks that do not produce extensive debris cover. As a result, relatively clean surface conditions on NOCA glaciers may lead to higher overall ablation than on glaciers with extensive debris cover, although shading and other factors are also important.

15

The large negative net mass balances observed on all four glaciers in water year 2009 were a product of average winter accumulation and above average summer melt. Net summer mass balance of Silver Glacier, and to a lesser extend Sandalee Glacier, was less negative than other glaciers due to their relatively high elevations and solar shading from Mount Spickard and McGregor Mountain, respectively.

The net volume loss from all four glaciers in 2009 was the third greatest since monitoring began, and was surpassed only during water years 2001 and 2005. Since 1993, the glaciers monitored have experienced a net decline in mass balance of about 22 M m^3 (566 B gallons).

Cumulative Balance

Between 1993 and 2009, 12 out of 17 years had negative net mass balances. Water year 2009 represented the seventh consecutive since 2003 where all four glaciers had negative net mass balances (Figure 3). This condition strengthened the strongly negative cumulative balance trend for all four glaciers. Since 1993, Noisy, North Klawatti, and Sandalee glaciers had cumulative net mass balances of about -15 m, whereas Silver Glacier had a cumulative balance of -9 m due to its height and north aspect (Figure 4).

The range in values of cumulative net mass balance for NOCA glaciers of – 16.7 to -9 m w.e. since 1993 are similar to those reported for adjacent South Cascade Glacier (Figure 4; McCabe and Fountain 1995), as well as glaciers at Mount Rainer and Olympic national parks within North Coast and Cascades Network (NCCN). At Mount Rainier, cumulative balance since 2003 is -8 m w.e. for Emmons Glacier and -9 m w.e. for Nisqually Glacier (Riedel and Larrabee, *in review*). Variability in cumulative balance is due to each glaciers unique relationship to local climate due to aspect, altitude range, shading, and secondary accumulation sources.

Glacier Remapping

Ten-year remapping of Sandalee and Silver glaciers was completed in 2009 and led to significant adjustment to the base maps used for integration of point (stake) measurement to the entire glacier surface. Both glaciers had net vertical surface decline exceeding 15 m. Back-adjustment of data from 2001-2009 with the new hypsometry data led to a significant decreases in cumulative balance of -3.30 m on Silver Glacier and -5.83 m on Sandalee Glacier.

Remapping shows that surface measurements tend to overestimate glacier mass balance, however, adjustment for NOCA glaciers are within the range of previous investigations (Conway et al. 1999, Krimmel 1999, Ostrem and Haakensen 1999, Andreasson 1999). Annual net mass balance decreased by an average -0.37 m w.e. and -0.65 m w.e. for Silver and Sandalee glaciers, respectively. These values are close to the average net mass balance measurement error of ±0.44 m and ±0.56 m for Silver and Sandalee glaciers.

In general, most of the cumulative loss from the four NOCA glaciers is in the ablation zone, or the lowest elevation part of a glacier. This is illustrated in figures 6, where Silver Glacier has lost as much as 15 m near its terminus. In contrast, Sandalee glacier has lost more mass in its accumulation zone because it is less well shaded than the lower glacier, which also receives accumulation from snow avalanche and wind redistribution (Figure 7).

Climate Controls on Mass Balance Trends and Variability

All of the metrics used to monitor glaciers as a Vital Sign at NOCA point to rapid loss of ice due to climate warming, which affects glaciers in several important ways (CIG 2004, IPCC 2007, Kovanen 2003, Mote 2003). Warmer temperatures increase the rate of summer melting and the length of the summer melt season. Summer melt in 2009 was the greatest since monitoring began at North Klawatti Glacier, second most at Noisy and Silver glaciers and third greatest at Sandalee Glacier. Since 1993 the average summer melt rate for all four glaciers has increased by about 12% (1m w.e.). A longer melt season comes at the expense of accumulation. Although no significant decrease in winter accumulation is observed in the mass balance data we believe that warm, late fall rains are causing some melt. Further, rain does not accumulate on the glacier to be transferred into glacial ice.

There are two important dimensions to rapid decline of glaciers at NOCA. At a seasonal timescale, warmer summers increase the rate of melt. This trend is offset to some extent by the longer timescale reduction in glacier area and volume. Thus while glaciers are delivering more water due to higher melt rates, their volume is being diminished. In the larger Skagit watershed, an average cumulative mass balance loss of -8 m since 2003 has led to a net loss of volume 400 B gallons of water. At an average daily discharge of about 10 B gallons, this represents a storage loss in the watershed equivalent to about one month's continuous flow of the Skagit River.

Long term variability in glacier net mass balance at NOCA is closely linked to inter-annual and decadal scale climate variability associated with El Nino-Southern Oscillation (ENSO) and the Pacific Decadal Oscillation (PDO) (McCabe and Fountain 1995, Hodge et al. 1997, Bitz and Battisti 1999). Extensive pools of cooler than normal water in the tropical Pacific (La Nina-phase ENSO) and cooler than normal sea surface temperatures in the eastern-central North Pacific Basin (cool-phase PDO) result in above normal precipitation and below normal melting of NOCA glaciers. Neither strong PDO nor ENSO forcing were observed in the glacial mass balance data in 2009. A run of positive mass water years between 1996 and 2002 reflected the last cool phase of the PDO.

Glacial Contribution to Streamflow

Glaciers provide substantial amounts of meltwater to several major rivers flowing from North Cascades National Park at a critical time of year. In four large rivers glaciers contributed approximately 472 M m^3 (121 B gallons) in water year 2009, which was above the 17 year average (Table 2).

The magnitude of glacial contribution to stream flow was large in 2009, but varied by the amount of glacial cover in each watershed and climate. In general, large watersheds on the wetter west slope of NOCA have more extensive glacial cover that produces a larger volume of glacial meltwater when compared to watersheds in the more arid eastern part of the park. However, glaciers produce a higher percent of runoff in the more arid Stehekin watershed because of less snowfall in general, making glacial buffering in arid climates on the east side of NOCA more critical.

Glaciers in Thunder Creek watershed, the most glaciated watershed in Washington at 12% ice cover, had the greatest contribution to summer runoff by volume and fraction of summer total at 165.7 M m3 and 44 percent, respectively. Glaciers in the Thunder Creek watershed contributed more than six times that as glaciers in the Ross Lake watershed, which has the smallest glacial area at one percent and contribution to total summer flow at seven percent (Table 2).

Glacial runoff estimates represent melt from ice, firn and snow accumulated on the glacier surfaces between about early April to later September. Measurement of the ice-only component of the melt was not made due to the time-transgressive start of the melt season on glaciers spanning 1000m in elevation, and a limited number of summer measurements on each glacier.

Literature Cited

Andreassen, L. M. 1999. Comparing traditional mass balance measurements with long-term volume change extracted from topographical maps: A case study of Storbreen glacier in Jotunheimen, Norway, for the period 1940-1997. *Geografiska Annaler* 81A:467-476.

Bitz, C. M., and D. S. Battisti. 1999. Interannual to decadal variability in climate and the glacier mass balance in Washington, Western Canada, and Alaska. *Journal of Climate* 12(11):3181-3196.

Climate Impacts Group (CIG). 2004. Overview of climate change impacts in the U.S. Pacific Northwest. Climate Impacts Group, Center for Science in the Earth System, Joint Institute for the Study of the Atmosphere and Ocean, University of Washington, Seattle.

Conway, H., L. Rasmussen, and H.-P. Marshall. 1999. Annual mass balance of Blue Glacier, USA: 1955–97. *Geografiska Annaler: Series A, Physical Geography* 81:509-520.

Granshaw, F. D., and A. G. Fountain. 2006. Glacier change (1958-1998) in the North Cascades National Park Complex, Washington, USA. *Journal of Glaciology* 52(177):251-256.

Hartzell, P. 2003. Glacial Ecology: North Cascades Glacier Macroinvertebrates (2002 Field Season). Online report: http://www.nichols.edu/departments/Glacier/2002.htm, last updated January 2003.

Hodge, S. M., D. C. Trabant, R. M. Krimmel, T. A. Heinrichs, R. S. March, and E. G. Josberger. 1998. Climate variations and changes in mass of three glaciers in western North America. *Journal of Climate* 11(9):2161-2179.

Intergovernmental Panel on Climate Change (IPCC). 2007. Climate Change 2007: Synthesis Report. Contribution of Working Groups I, II and III to the Fourth Assessment Report of the Intergovernmental Panel on Climate Change. IPCC, Geneva, Switzerland.

Krimmel, R. M. 1994. Water, ice and meteorological measurements at South Cascade Glacier, Washington, 1993 Balance Year. Water-Resources Investigations Report 94-4139. U.S. Geological Survey, Tacoma, Washington.

Krimmel, R. M. 1995. Water, ice and meteorological measurements at South Cascade Glacier, Washington, 1994 Balance Year. Water-Resources Investigations Report 95-4139. U.S. Geological Survey, Tacoma, Washington.

Krimmel, R. M. 1996. Water, ice and meteorological measurements at South Cascade Glacier, Washington, 1995 Balance Year. Water-Resources Investigations Report 96-4139. U.S. Geological Survey, Tacoma, Washington.

Krimmel, R. M. 1996a. Glacier mass balance using the grid-index method. Pages 62-68 *in* S. C. Colbeck, ed. Glaciers, ice sheets and volcanoes: A tribute to Mark F. Meier: U.S. Army Corps of Engineers Cold Region Research and Engineering Laboratory Special Report 96-27.

Krimmel, R. M. 1999. Analysis of difference between direct and geodetic mass balance measurements at South Cascade Glacier, Washington. *Geografiska Annaler: Series A, Physical Geography* 81:653-658.

Kovanen, D. J. 2003. Decadal variability in climate and glacier fluctuations on Mt. Baker, Washington, U.S.A. *Geografiska Annaler: Series A, Physical Geography* 85: 43–55.

Mayo, L. R., M. F. Meier, and W. V. Tangborn. 1972. A system to combine stratigraphic and annual mass-balance systems: A contribution to the International Hydrological Decade. *Journal of Glaciology* 11(61):3-14.

McCabe, G. J., and A. F. Fountain. 1995. Relations between atmospheric circulation and mass balance of South Cascade Glacier, Washington, U.S.A. *Arctic and Alpine Research* 27(3):226-233.

Meier, M. F. 1961. Mass budget of South Cascade Glacier, 1957-1960. U.S. Geological Survey Professional Paper 424-B. U.S. Geological Survey, Tacoma, Washington.

Meier, M. F., and W. V. Tangborn. 1965. Net budget and flow of South Cascade Glacier, Washington. *Journal of Glaciology* 5(41):547-566.

Meier, M. F., L. R. Mayo, and A. L. Post. 1971. Combined ice and water balances of Gulkana and Wolverine Glaciers, Alaska, and South Cascade Glacier, Washington, 1965 and 1966 hydrologic years. U.S. Geological Survey Professional Paper 715-A. U.S. Geological Survey, Tacoma, Washington.

Mote, P. W. 2003. Trends in temperature and precipitation in the Pacific Northwest during the twentieth century. *Northwest Science* 77(4):271-282.

Ostrem, G., and A. Stanley. 1969. Glacier mass balance measurements - a manual for field and office measurements. The Canadian Department of Energy, Mines and Resources, and the Norwegian Water Resources and Electricity Board.

Ostrem, G., and M. Brugman. 1991. Glacier mass balance measurements: A manual for field and office work. National Hydrology Research Institute, Inland Waters Directorate, Conservation and Protection Science Report No. 4. Environment Canada, Saskatoon, Saskatchewan, Canada.

Ostrem, G., and N. Haakensen. 1999. Map comparison of traditional mass-balance measurements: Which method is better? *Geografiska Annaler. Series A* 81A (4):703-11.

Paterson, W. S. B. 1981. The Physics of Glaciers. Pergamon Press, Elmsford, New York.

Pelto, M. S., and J. L. Riedel. 2001. Spatial and Temporal Variations in Annual Balance of North Cascade Glaciers, Washington 1984-2000. *Hydrologic Processes* 15:3461-3472.

Riedel, J. L, R. A Burrows, and J. M. Wenger. 2008. Long term monitoring of small glaciers at North Cascades National Park: A prototype park model for the North Coast and Cascades

Network. Natural Resource Report NPS/NCCN/NRR – 2008/066. U.S. National Park Service, Fort Collins, Colorado.

Riedel, J., and M. A. Larrabee. *In Review*. Mount Rainier National Park Annual Glacier Mass Balance Monitoring, Water Year 2009, North Coast and Cascades Network. Natural Resource Technical Report NPS/NCCN/NRTR—2011/XXX. National Park Service, Fort Collins, Colorado.

Tangborn, W. V., R. M. Krimmel, and M. F. Meier. 1971. A comparison of glacier mass balance by glaciological, hydrological, and mapping methods, South Cascade Glacier, Washington. Snow and Ice Symposium, IAHS-AISH Publication no. 104.

NPS 168/109433, August 2011

www.ingramcontent.com/pod-product-compliance
Lightning Source LLC
Chambersburg PA
CBHW080739290526
45790CB00008B/3252